# This book belongs to:

_____

_____

This book is designed to encourage small children to talk about what they see in the colorful pictures. Some simple questions have been suggested, but many more can be made up.

Always try to find a quiet space to share this book with your child. Children will be generous with their responses if you encourage them and give them confidence. They learn new words quickly and love to use them. A good vocabulary helps them think and enables them to express their thoughts.

Most important, enjoy the book together.

Written by Kath Jewitt
Illustrated by Claire Henley
Language consultant: Betty Root

This edition published by Parragon in 2007

Parragon Publishing
Queen Street House
4 Queen Street
Bath, BA1 1HE, UK
Copyright © Parragon Books Ltd 2005

ISBN 978-1-4075-0348-6
Printed in Indonesia

# My First Book of...

# DIGGERS
### and
# DUMP TRUCKS

p

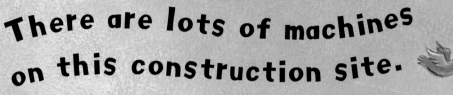

There are lots of machines on this construction site.

Can you point to all
the different ones?

# Do you know what these machines are called?

digger

dump truck

rock breaker

steamroller

# Point to each one and say its name.

bulldozer                    cement mixer

crane

This digger is working hard on the construction site.

# What is it doing?

# Here is a dump truck
# with a heavy load.

# What is happening in this picture?

The bulldozer is moving some heavy rocks.

# Find another bulldozer in the picture.

This machine is called
a rock breaker.
It has a special arm.

The rock breaker uses its arm to break big rocks into small ones.

Can you point to the small rocks?

A cement mixer
mixes up cement.

# This crane has a long arm to lift heavy things.

# What is happening in this picture?

This machine uses its heavy roller to flatten the ground.

Can you remember what it is called?

People drive the machines on the construction site.

Point to the drivers
in this picture.

What are the other
workers doing?

The digger is yellow.
The bulldozer is green.

# Find the red and blue machines in this picture.

# What are all the machines doing?